Original title:
The Citrus Symphony

Author: Colin Leclair
ISBN HARDBACK: 978-1-80586-413-4
ISBN PAPERBACK: 978-1-80586-885-9

Nature’s Citrus Chorus

In a grove where lemons play,
Oranges dance the night away,
Limes are juggling, what a sight,
Underneath the moon so bright.

Grapefruits giggle, bouncing round,
With citrus tunes, a lively sound,
Tangerines hold hands and spin,
While sour notes begin to grin.

A lemon slide, oh what a thrill,
High-flying zest, they climb the hill,
With every squirt, a burst of cheer,
Citrus laughter, loud and clear.

In this orchard, joy’s not lost,
Each fruit a friend, no matter cost,
With peels that shine like sunny rays,
Together they sing, all on display.

Saffron and Citrus

In a garden bright, fruits sing,
Lemons dance, while oranges swing.
Saffron dreams of a fruity fate,
With every zest, they celebrate.

Limes play hopscotch, oh so spry,
Grapefruits giggle, reaching high.
Citrus pranks in sunny rays,
Saffron chuckles, lost in plays.

Orchard Melodies

In orchards wide, the colors clash,
Bananas giggle with a splash.
Tangerines toss jokes in the breeze,
While plump peaches sway with ease.

Every fruit finds their tone,
Singing loudly, never alone.
Melodies drip from trees above,
In this fruity world, all is love.

Citrus Rainsong

When it rains, oh what a sight,
Juicy splashes, pure delight.
Pineapples sing a rainy tune,
As raindrops dance, oh what a boon!

Lemons slide, a comical sight,
While oranges giggle, feeling bright.
Each drop's a note, in nature's score,
A citrus choir, we must adore.

The Vibrant Palette of Citrus

In a palette wild, colors burst,
Citrus antics quench our thirst.
Limes and lemons, orange delight,
Painting joy in morning light.

With zest and giggles, flavors play,
A fruity feast to start the day.
Every bite, a canvas bright,
In this banquet, all feels right.

Harmonies in Every Slice

Lemons dance with a twist,
In a bowl, they party and jest.
Limes jump in, with a zing,
Together, they form a zest.

Oranges sing a fruity tune,
Squeezed joy spills in the afternoon.
Their laughter echoes through the air,
As citrus friends spread good cheer everywhere.

Citrus Delight

Grapefruit wears a dazzling grin,
As tangy jokes swirl within.
Tangerines toss peels on the floor,
Creating smiles, oh what a score!

Mimosas wink with bubbly grace,
Join the zestful, lively race.
All the fruits, in a jolly brawl,
Roll on, roll off, they have a ball!

Festive Citrus Revelry

Citrus hats on every head,
Dancing fruits, so brightly bred.
Lemon drops and limey hops,
A frolicking feast that never stops.

With every slice, a joke unfolds,
In juicy tales, laughter molds.
Citrus wonders, a playful spree,
Bringing giggles, oh so free!

Vibrant Citrus Portraits

Citrus brush strokes, oh so bold,
Painting laughter to unfold.
Lemon-lime, such vibrant hues,
Crafting giggles as my muse.

Tropical breezes carry the sound,
Of fruity fun playing all around.
In this portrait, love runs wild,
Each zestful fruit, a joyful child.

Orchards in Bloom

In orchards bright, the fruits collide,
A lemon laughs, a lime will slide.
They dance around, a wacky scene,
With orange balls where squirrels convene.

A grapefruit sings a silly tune,
While tangerines take off by noon.
They trade their hats for big sun glasses,
And giggle as the harvest passes.

Symphony of Flavors

A zesty orchestra in a bowl,
With jolly notes that tease the soul.
The tangy strings are finely tuned,
As limes and lemons get marooned.

A banjo made of citrus peel,
Plucks funny melodies that feel,
Like sunshine rays on summer's feet,
A fruity symphony, oh so sweet.

Citrus Breezes

The breezes bring a citrus hum,
As orangutans play drums that thrum.
Limes fling jokes at the passing pears,
While grapefruits roll down the stairs.

The wind whispers through lemon trees,
Tickling the leaves with citrus breeze.
In every twist, a laugh is found,
As zesty spirits whirl around.

Vibrant Sun-kissed Melodies

The sun-kissed fruits burst into song,
With vibrant notes that can't go wrong.
Lemonade wishes float through the air,
As fruits unite without a care.

A joyful mix of colors bright,
Sway in rhythm, left and right.
Each citrus slice, a giggling shout,
Makes everyone want to dance about.

Lemon's Laughter

When life gives you lemons, just grin wide,
Make a funny face, let joy reside.
Sour sneers turn sweet in a zesty whirl,
Lemonade giggles make the best world.

Zesty yellow orbs roll on the floor,
Slipping and sliding, oh, hear them roar!
Tell all the puns, let laughter ignite,
Citrus chuckles shine so bright.

Grapefruit Gala

In a frosty bowl, they dance with glee,
Colorful halves, oh can't you see?
A fruity fiesta, with hats made of rind,
Sipping grapefruit juice, one of a kind.

They toss around jokes, in juicy delight,
Sour or sweet, they don't put up a fight.
Just watch as they twirl, in their sugary show,
At the grapefruit gala, everyone's the pro.

The Squeeze of Harmony

A citrus choir sings, with zestful flair,
Lemons on trumpets, limes in the air.
Mandarins whirl like a merry-go-round,
In the squeeze of harmony, joy's abound.

Peeling back laughter, a cheerful sound,
The tangy treble makes the world round.
With a splash of juice and a dash of cheer,
Citrus serenades, bring us near.

Citrus Color Palette

A palette of fruit, in bright yellow hues,
Splashing around in a jolly blues cruise.
Oranges giggle, as they patter and twirl,
Painting the canvas, oh what a swirl!

With greenish tints, the limes lend their zest,
In this citrus circus, it’s truly the best.
A burst of color, a comical spree,
Joyfully splashed, so vibrant and free.

Aromatic Citrus Rhapsody

In clouds of zest, we dance, we twirl,
Orange peels in a fruity whirl!
Lemons giggle, oh what a cheer,
Making lemonade with a playful sneer.

Grapefruits bounce on the kitchen floor,
Sour dances, who could ask for more?
Tangy tunes in the summer sun,
A raucous feast, oh what fun!

Juicy Echoes

A lime rolls by with a sassy shout,
“Zesty whispers, come try it out!”
Citrus laughter fills the air,
In every fruit, there's joy to share.

Tangerines sing on the branch so bright,
Dancing in the warm daylight.
With every squeeze, the giggles grow,
Juicy echoes in the row!

The Essence of Orchard Dreams

In orchards grand, we laugh and sway,
Peeling memories, come what may.
Lemonade puddles fill the lane,
Slipping and sliding, oh what a gain!

Grapes in capes say, 'Join the spree!'
Fruity pranks are wild and free.
Juggling fruits with a cheerful grin,
A juicy party, let’s begin!

Citrus Polka

Twirl with oranges, twist with zest,
A polka party, oh how we jest!
Lemons do the tango with flare,
In this juicy dance, we have no care.

Pomelos leap like frogs in the sun,
With every hop, there's laughter to be spun.
Citrus tunes in a jangly beat,
Swinging and swaying in fruity heat!

Zesty Rhythms

In the orchard, fruits do dance,
Lemons prance in bright expanse.
Oranges juggle on a spree,
Mangoes laugh, oh can't you see?

Grapefruits hum a funny tune,
Limes are mood swings, but in June.
Each fruit's got a wacky beat,
Underneath the sun's warm seat.

Tasting joys in every bite,
Juicy laughs, such pure delight.
Peels and rinds toss in the air,
A citrus party, free of care.

Wrap your tongue in tangy fun,
Zesty jokes, there's always one.
Life's a sketch, with colors bright,
In the orchard's funny light.

Orchard’s Whispering Wind

Whispers float on breezy notes,
Limes debate on silly quotes.
Tangerines roll with delight,
Their giggles fill the sunny height.

Branches sway, fruits trade their jokes,
Grapefruits bounce like silly folks.
Each breeze brings a citrus glee,
A fruity laugh for you and me.

Lemonade stands in a row,
Squeezing out puns, watch them glow.
Sour and sweet, they mix and match,
In the wind, the stories hatch.

With a twist and a citrus grin,
Every fruit earns a playful win.
Let the orchard’s laughter blend,
A tasty tune that has no end.

Tangerine Tones

Notes of tangerine fill the air,
Funky fruit, without a care.
In this grove, puns reign supreme,
Oranges dance in a wacky dream.

Lemon drops with a silly sway,
Limes do cartwheels in joyful play.
Grapefruits tease with a spin and flip,
Join the fruit parade on a citrus trip.

Each flavor sings a quirky rhyme,
Adding sweetness to our time.
Jokes collide in every taste,
In this medley, none goes to waste.

So bite a slice, embrace the song,
Fruity fun where you belong.
With laughter ripe in every tone,
In this garden, joy has grown.

Vibrant Citrus Canvas

Brush of zest on vibrant shades,
Citrus laughter never fades.
Painted peels and halos bright,
In the market, pure delight.

Orange strokes with cheerful flair,
Tangerine twirls in the air.
Lemon lines, so crisp and real,
Crafting smiles with every peel.

Fruitful colors splash and blend,
This is how the jokes transcend.
From the orchard, art does spring,
In every slice, we taste and sing.

So hang this canvas on your wall,
With citrus jokes that stand up tall.
Let laughter drip in every hue,
A vibrant world just waits for you.

Golden Zest Reverie

In a grove where lemons dance,
Limes play tag with sweet romance.
Oranges giggle, bouncing high,
As tangerines just roll on by.

A grapefruit sings a silly tune,
While juicing up the afternoon.
Mandarins wear hats of cheer,
Inviting all the folks to hear.

Pineapples wear sunglasses bright,
As coconuts join in the fight.
They duel with zest, not a care,
Making laughter fill the air.

So let’s toast to this fruity crew,
With drinks that spark, and smiles anew.
In this land where laughter flows,
Citrus joy is all that grows.

Sunshine's Fruity Notes

Mangoes wiggle in a line,
Practicing for the showtime shine.
Kiwi shrugs and does a spin,
While bananas wear goofy grins.

Peaches leap with joyful zest,
Bouncing in a fruity fest.
Lemons blare their trumpet loud,
Creating laughs that draw a crowd.

A zesty jig that never quits,
With each sweet drop, the fun commits.
Fruits sing songs from every tree,
In harmony, wild and free.

So let's join in this sunny glee,
As every fruit dances with spree.
The notes are bright, the mood so light,
In this fruity world of pure delight.

Citrus Tempos of Happiness

Lemons strolling with a flair,
Dancing like they haven't a care.
Limes take steps that turn the tide,
With oranges bouncing side by side.

In this grove of bumbling fun,
Chasing sunshine, on the run.
Pomelos cheer, their laughter loud,
As grapefruits gather a smiling crowd.

A citrus band, all dressed in green,
Strumming tunes that make us beam.
Pineapple plays the ukulele,
While cherries shine, all yellow and jolly.

So join the beat, don’t miss the show,
With every twist, the joy will grow.
In this citrus world so bright,
Happiness dances, pure delight.

Tropical Citrus Whirls

In a world where grapefruits glide,
With playful tricks they cannot hide.
Oranges twirl in fruity gowns,
Creating giggles all around.

Tropical breezes sway and hum,
As limes perform a silly drum.
Coconuts roll, adding to the beat,
With each tiny hop, oh, what a feat!

Bananas swing in silly pairs,
While lemons stretch without a care.
A fruity whirl of laughter bright,
Echoes through the starry night.

So let's join hands, take a chance,
In this zesty, crazy dance.
With every laugh, the fruit we twirl,
In this rich, wonderful citrus world.

Citrus Waltz

Lemons dance in sunny rays,
Twisting round in cheerful plays.
Oranges giggle in the breeze,
Swinging low among the trees.

Limes are laughing, full of zest,
Juggling sweetness, they're the best.
Grapefruits frolic, bold and bright,
Twirling under moon's soft light.

Mandarins put on a show,
Prancing high, oh what a glow!
With each twist, they spill their juice,
Making everyone let loose!

Citrus party, what a blast,
Every moment flies so fast.
Squeeze the day, it's juicy fun,
In this waltz, we've just begun!

The Sweet Symphony of Life

Pineapples hum a silly song,
Bouncing on the beats so strong.
Kiwi winks with playful glee,
Joining in this fruity spree.

Bananas slip with funky flair,
Charming every cheerful pair.
Strawberries flip like acrobats,
Hats off to the flying bats!

Ripe avocados join the beat,
Making every corner sweet.
Peaches giggle, feeling bold,
Spreading joy like tales of old.

In this symphony, we sway,
Fruits and fun come out to play.
Life's a treat, so don't you fret,
Join the laughter, you'll forget!

Orchard’s Bounty

In the orchard, fruits collide,
Smiles and giggles, what a ride!
Citrus characters abound,
Tickling toes upon the ground.

With each pluck, a burst of joy,
Citrus zest, like every toy.
Trees are chuckling in the air,
Sharing secrets everywhere.

Cherries chime a happy tune,
Lemons bounce from noon to moon.
Grapes are rolling down the slopes,
Filling all with juicy hopes.

In this bounty, laughter grows,
Fruitful moments, sweet like prose.
Pick a laugh, just take a bite,
Every flavor feels so right!

Citron Serenade

Underneath the sun's warm glow,
Citrons sing, putting on a show.
Juggling flavors, here and there,
Each a note in fruity air.

Tangerines tap dance with flair,
Orange spritz fills up the air.
Lemons laugh with zestful cheer,
Joining in to spread the beer!

Limes and grapefruits form a band,
Playing tunes, oh isn't it grand?
In this serenade, we sway,
Fruits and giggles lead the way!

Join the throng, take a chance,
Let the citrus make you dance.
In this jig, we find our pride,
Come together, side by side!

Zesty Rhapsody

Lemons dance in sunny hats,
Twirling 'round with silly chats.
Oranges giggle, sharing jokes,
While grapefruits play with sly, sweet folks.

Limes roll by in neon shoes,
Sipping juice and singing blues.
Pomelos pop, they can't keep still,
Bouncing high with zest and thrill.

Citrus clouds in lemon skies,
Peeling laughter, oh, what a surprise!
Satsumas join with a cheeky grin,
Chewing gum with sour skin.

A tangerine tells a punny tale,
While kumquats dance without fail.
In this grove, the fruit’s all fun,
Hearts are bright, brighter than the sun.

A Medley of Tang

Tangerines in big, bright hats,
Juggling oranges, fancy spats.
Lemons leap, oh what a sight,
Citrus giggles, pure delight.

Limes do cartwheels, what a flair!
Making juice fly everywhere.
Sipping tea in silly cups,
Grapefruit jokes? They crack us up!

In the orchard, fun's the tone,
Where tangy fruits can call home.
Every peel, a punchline sweet,
With every drink, we can't be beat.

Fruits in glasses clink with cheer,
Join the dance, come one, come near!
Taste the laughter, feel the zing,
In this tangy, fruity fling!

Citrus Crescendo

In orchards bright, fruits tangle and tease,
Squeezing laughter like a twist of breeze.
Limes make jokes that roll and twirl,
As oranges spin in a joy-filled whirl.

Lemons sing with zesty flair,
While grapefruits share tales with a flair.
Satsumas giggle, they're quite the hit,
Throwing punches with every wit.

A lemon’s grin can brighten the day,
Making sour times melt away.
Kumquats chant in quirky beat,
As touchy tangerines dance on their feet.

Together they form a symphonic jest,
In this fruity fest, we feel our best!
Raise your glass and join the fun,
This citrus party’s just begun!

Notes from the Orchard

Peeling our laughter, oh what a sound,
Dancing fruit legends in a circle round.
Limes throw confetti from the tree,
While lemons giggle in harmony.

The oranges prance in a mischievous way,
Squeaking tunes that brighten the day.
Grapefruits roll with a playful bounce,
Their jokes just seem to always flounce.

As twilight falls, the citrus crew,
Swaps stories as night slips through.
With every toast, a juicy cheer,
Fruity melodies fill the air!

In every slice, a tale is spun,
Orchard vibes of pure, fruity fun.
So join us here, you'll never regret,
In this tangy world, there's no fret!

Orchard Overture

In the grove where lemons laugh,
Limes play jokes and chase each other.
Oranges roll like playful calves,
While grapefruits gossip with fervor.

A tangerine hops on a pear,
Singing songs of zesty delight.
Citrus friends dance without a care,
Their bright smiles shine oh so bright.

A lime squeezed into a joke,
Said, "I'm zestier than you think!"
But oranges retorted, without choke,
"You're just sour, give us a wink!"

They hold a party under the sun,
With spritz and laughter all around.
It's a citrus bash, oh what fun!
Where zingy notes are joy unbound.

Rind and Rapture

In a vibrant patch, the fruits engage,
The mandarin tells tales of zest.
Watermelons get off the stage,
Claiming, "Juicy is simply the best!"

A clever grapefruit knits a hat,
For a lemon tired of the heat.
They giggle at the slapstick spat,
As oranges dance on tiny feet.

Limes are labeled as the class clown,
Peeling jokes that take their toll.
Each punchline makes the others frown,
But laughter's always in control.

A citrus fair, all jokes aside,
Where friendship's flavor fills the air.
They joyfully sing with citrus pride,
In a raucous, zesty affair!

Juicy Reverberations

Bouncing into the orchard bright,
Cherries clash with sweet surprise.
Fruits spin round in pure delight,
As laughter ripples through the skies.

An orange tried to play a tune,
But lemons outshine with their zest.
Yet grapefruits crooned a lovely croon,
While dancing like they'd won a quest.

A passionfruit took to the stage,
With all the bravado it could muster.
"Check my moves, I'm all the rage!"
But tripped on juice and turned to fluster.

Each note a burst of citrus cheer,
Where mischief mingles with the fun.
With giggles shared, the mood sincere,
An orchard concert 'neath the sun!

Sunlit Citrus Dance

Underneath the warm sun's glow,
Citrus pals put on a show.
Lemon twirled, a lemony whirl,
While everyone laughed at the swirl.

Limes in tuxedos, oh so posh,
Appeared to prance in dapper wash.
An orange juggles with such flair,
As grapefruits play the silly pair.

Peeling jokes that fly around,
With splashes fresh and laughs unbound.
A dance-off greets the midday sun,
In sweet, zany fun, they run.

Now in joy, they prance and reel,
In this crazy citrus ideal.
With every skit and every glance,
The orchard blooms in a sunny dance!

Breezes of Juicy Fragrance

In a garden where lemons laugh,
Oranges dance in a citrus half.
Lime trees chuckle with playful glee,
As every fruit hums, 'You can't catch me!'

Grapefruits roll like giddy balls,
While tangerines dodge and do the sprawls.
A breeze of zest tickles the air,
With each squeeze, joy’s everywhere!

Lemons wear hats and twirl around,
While limes laugh loudly, oh such a sound!
Even the pith swings with delight,
In this fruity world, what a sight!

So here’s to breezes, so light and pure,
With every squeeze, forever endure.
Join the laughter, come take a ride,
In this juicy realm, let’s all collide!

Orange Blossoms in Bloom

Orange blossoms giggle in the sun,
Wobbling in shades, oh, what a run!
Petals spin like tops in a race,
Chasing the bees in a silly chase.

The breeze whispers secrets to the trees,
While bouncing fruits laugh like best buddies.
Lemonade dreams float in the air,
Making everyone stop and stare.

Twirling branches with a citrus grin,
Joking around, it’s all part of the win.
Even the roots have their chuckle fit,
In this fragrant place, why not commit?

So come and join this floral ballet,
Where blossoms and fruits dance every day.
With petals and laughter that fills the room,
Revelry blossoms forever in bloom!

Serenade of Citrusy Skies

Under skies of tangy delights,
Fruit-folk gather for giggly heights.
Clouds shaped like lemons float by,
With laughter that makes the sun sigh.

Tangerines sing with voices so sweet,
While orange slices tap their feet.
Each note glides on a tarty breeze,
Lifting spirits like zesty leaves.

Marmalade dreams take to the air,
As juice drops tumble without a care.
Magic sprinkles from way up high,
In this citrus tale that makes us sigh.

So sway with the rhythm, let’s take a chance,
Join the fruits in their joyous dance.
In the serenade of flavors that fly,
We’ll laugh and twirl under citrusy sky!

Sunkissed Symphony

In the land where sunlight meets the zest,
Fruits gather round for a juicy fest.
Watermelons waddle, and lemons jest,
Citrus giggles, it's simply the best!

A harp made of peel plucks sweet notes,
While oranges wear hats and colorful coats.
The melody pops with the splash of bright,
As citrusy snail plays, "Take it light!"

Peach and plum join in a funky beat,
As ripe bananas get up on their feet.
Dancing green limes, what a hilarious sight,
Sunkissed symphony, pure delight!

So let's raise a toast to this sunny crew,
A toast of fresh juice, and we'll sing too.
With laughter and melody, life's never grim,
In a world where every fruit can swim!

Rhapsody of Ripe Citrus

In the orchard, lemons grin,
Swaying slowly, they begin.
Oranges giggle, bright and round,
Happiness in every sound.

Limes are bouncing in their beds,
Tickling ants upon their heads.
Tangerines dance, oh what a sight,
Spreading joy in the golden light.

Peeling laughter fills the air,
As fruits wear hats without a care.
Join the fun, come take a seat,
Swirling flavors, oh so sweet!

In this grove, we share a joke,
With juicy fruit, the laughter's woke.
Quirky sprites with citrus zest,
In this rhapsody, we are blessed.

Juicy Whispers in the Grove

Whispers swirl beneath the trees,
Murmuring secrets with the breeze.
Grapefruit giggles, plump and bright,
Juicy tales of day and night.

Lemonade ducks quack with glee,
Frolicking near a zesty spree.
Limes are rolling, trying to keep,
Chasing each other in a leap!

Pineapple dreams in sunny rays,
Draw circles in the orchard bays.
Tasting honey from the pine,
Join the laughter, it's divine!

In citrus whispers, humor brews,
With every joke, a citrus muse.
Bouncing jokes, oh sweet delight,
Juicy giggles, day and night.

The Sweetness of Sunlit Citrus

Sun-kissed fruits in the warm embrace,
Wobble and wiggle in this place.
Grapes applaud in tangled vines,
Chortling sweetly, oh how they shine!

Orange balloons float through the air,
Tickling bees with a fruity flair.
Lemon drops roll down the hill,
Chasing laughter, heartbeats thrill.

Tangerine twirls on a merry spree,
Cartwheeling wildly, oh can’t you see?
Fruity giggles fill the sky,
As jolly fruits watch time fly by.

In this sweetness, we will bask,
With slices, jokes, and tales to ask.
Laughter ripens with every bite,
Under the sun, everything’s bright!

Grapefruit Ballad

In a bowl, the grapefruits sway,
Singing tunes in a zesty way.
Juicy ballads fill the air,
As fruits share tales beyond compare.

Dancing skins of pink and green,
Flavored giggles, quite the scene.
Ripe fruit jesters in a line,
Swap banter with the summer shine.

Bouncing berries join the mix,
Challenging grapefruits with their tricks.
Who can dance the twisty way?
Laughter echoes, come and play!

In this ballad, humor reigns,
With zesty notes and sweet refrains.
Join the fun, don't miss the beat,
Together here, life is sweet!

Harmony of the Orchard's Heart.

In a grove, the laughter swells,
Fruits giggle as the sunlight yells.
Lemons dance with silly grace,
While oranges roll in a fruity race.

Bouncing berries join the show,
Twirling peels in a citrus flow.
Sweet tangerines crack jokes so bright,
As limes juggle under the starry light.

Grapefruits sing with voices loud,
Creating chaos in the crowd.
Together they form a merry choir,
A zesty tune that climbs up higher.

In this orchard, joy takes flight,
Where fruits unite in pure delight.
With every note, the flavors blend,
Citrus fun that never ends.

Oranges in the Moonlight

Under the moon’s bright, silver gleam,
Oranges sway, they giggle and beam.
With playful whispers, they take a chance,
Inviting everyone to join the dance.

Grapes roll in, trying to compete,
But stumble and land at their fruity feet.
In the glow, limes wear tiny hats,
And lemons throw confetti at chubby cats.

They sing about juice and tangy zest,
While flying fruits invite the best.
Every citrus star shines like a dream,
In the laughter of the orchard's scheme.

As shadows play the night’s last game,
Fruits feast on joy, not on fame.
With a wink, they promise more laughs,
In the orchard where humor ever drafts.

Melodies of Zest

Zesty tunes in the afternoon,
With citrus crooners, a fruity tune.
Mangoes strum on guitar strings,
Coconuts join with the joy that sings.

Lemons leap in high, bright cheers,
While oranges share silly fears.
With each joke, their spirits soar,
Making the orchard a fun galore.

As bananas slip on the mossy ground,
Limes laugh hard at the sight they found.
Squirrels join in, with merry play,
In this citrus world, hip-hip-hooray!

The zest fills the air, a fizzy delight,
Where fruits share joy 'til the morning light.
In this vibrant, fruity mist,
A comedy show no one can resist.

Citrus Echoes of Spring

Spring awakens with a fruity cheer,
As lemons giggle, 'We're finally here!'
They tickle blossoms, sprouting up wide,
With jokes and pranks, all fruits aside.

Oranges juggle blooming flowers,
While grapefruits boast of juicy powers.
In the breeze, a tangerine shout,
'Watch us laugh, that's what we're about!'

Banter fills the sunny air,
Mirth and mischief everywhere.
In this citrus carnival of spring,
Every taste and laughter they bring.

As buds unfold, the giggles grow,
In this orchard, pure fun flows.
With peels and puns, the echo sings,
Celebrating life and all it brings.

Squeeze of Sweetness

In the orchard, a dance of delight,
Lemons giggle, oh what a sight.
Oranges waltz with a zestful cheer,
While limes swirl, spreading joy near.

A grapefruit juggles in the sun,
Fruit salad parties, oh what fun!
Sours and sweets in a merry prance,
Join the laughter, come take a chance.

Tangerines tumble, rolling away,
In citrus chaos, we all play.
With peels like confetti, oh what a throw,
This juicy jubilee steals the show.

Citrus critters share silly tales,
About pithy pirates and their gales.
In this grove, there's no frown allowed,
Just fruity giggles, loud and proud.

Harmony of Zesty Dreams

Lemons strut in a choo-choo train,
While oranges whistle in rhythm of rain.
Limes tap dance on a sweet tango beat,
Peeling laughter that's hard to defeat.

Satsumas whisper their secrets so bright,
Under the moon, they twinkle at night.
Grapefruits grumble with silly prose,
Sharing zesty dreams that nobody knows.

Pineapples chuckle, their tops held high,
Chasing each other under the sky.
With colors and flavors all around,
In this harmony, pure joy is found.

Citrus carousel spins wild and free,
Round and round, come join the spree.
With a dash of fun, we make our way,
In the land of zest, we'll laugh and play.

Lemonade Lullaby

Sipping sweet nectar, oh what a dream,
Lemonade giggles, a fizzy gleam.
Sipping slow, with a cheeky grin,
Citrusy whispers invite us in.

Bubbles bounce in a glassy parade,
Wiggling limes join the lemonade.
The strawberries blush at the joke of the day,
Join in this chorus, come laugh and play.

Ice cubes clink in a funny tune,
While mint leaves sway under the moon.
Fizzy concoctions burst with cheer,
A lemonade lullaby, oh so dear.

Cheers to the humor in every sip,
As flavors tango and dance on the lip.
With lemons and laughter, we toast tonight,
In this zesty adventure, everything's right.

Tang of Twilight

As the sun starts to sink low,
Oranges wink in a golden glow.
Limes giggle as shadows begin,
Twilight's tangy humor draws us in.

In the evening, the fruits come alive,
Mellow murmurs and laughter survive.
Pineapples prance in the dusky hush,
While berries blush and the evenings rush.

A citrus serenade fills the air,
With zesty tunes, laughter to share.
Grapefruits spin tales of tropical flights,
While starry skies sprinkle funny sights.

In this dance of the night so bright,
We sip on dreams till the morning light.
With zestful joy, we'll twirl and sway,
In the tang of twilight, come out and play.

Flavors of the Golden Hour

In the sky, oranges fly,
Lemon clouds rush on by.
Grapefruit giggles in the breeze,
While tangerines dance with glee.

Sunsets serve a zesty drink,
Lime and laughter, what do you think?
Every sip, a chuckle abounds,
In this fruity world, joy resounds.

Chasing flavors of the bright,
Peeling laughter, pure delight.
Sipping shadows on the ground,
As zesty melodies are found.

Even the oranges like to play,
Making puns in their citrus way.
Golden hour, a fruity show,
Where every slice can steal the show.

Harmonies of Citrus Colors

Lemon lights on the stage,
Orange jests take the wage.
Bouncing tunes of lime and zest,
In this band, we are the best.

Grapefruit strums the mellow notes,
Tarts and sweets in silly coats.
Witty rhymes in citrus code,
Every chorus brings a road.

Surprises in every peel,
Can you handle all this real?
Harmony from pulp and rind,
A giggle echoing, you’ll find.

Bask in tunes of tangy cheer,
As fruits unite with all good beer.
In this grand citrus chime,
We laugh and dance, it's fruit time!

Sweet Citrus Adventures

Travel through an orange maze,
Finding giggles, sunny rays.
Peeling joy in zesty fun,
Chasing rays, we run and run.

Lemon trails and tangerine,
Adventures sweet, a fruity scene.
Jokes aside, what's next to taste?
Hilarity, I won't waste!

Whirling 'round in a juicy spin,
Sour faces, we won't let in.
Bouncing flavors everywhere,
Join our citrus laughter affair!

Every twist comes with a grin,
A hilarious citrus win.
Love the zest and love each bite,
In this orchard, pure delight!

Citrus Carols of the Heart

Singing songs of lemon light,
Carols sparkle, oh so bright.
Grapefruit harmonies unfold,
While the oranges spin tales bold.

In this choir, we find our cheer,
With every peel, we persevere.
Chanting rhythms sweet and sour,
In this fruit-filled, happy hour.

Tangerine tunes, oh what a sight,
Citrus laughter, pure delight.
Under stars of limey hue,
We sing of joy, all night through.

With each verse, a citrus cheer,
Let's spread laughter, far and near.
In our hearts, this fruit will spark,
The passion of a summertime lark.

Lemonade Symphony

In a pitcher, yellow smiles,
Sour notes dance for miles.
Sugar joins the lively tune,
Sipping sun beneath the moon.

Lemon slices wear tiny hats,
Straws wiggle like friendly cats.
Each gulp a bubbly serenade,
Who knew joy was freshly made?

Frogs jump in with zestful croaks,
While giggling, we share our jokes.
The ice cubes jingle, keep it cool,
Lemonade, oh what a fool!

When life hands you tangy fruit,
Grab a glass, don't be astute.
A citrus giggle in each sip,
Fun unfolds, let laughter rip!

Mandarins in the Mist

Mandarins hang like Christmas lights,
Beneath the fog, they spark delight.
Peeling laughter fills the air,
Juice drips down without a care.

In the mist, oranges play hide-and-seek,
Witty whispers make these fruits unique.
Their zest is bold, their humor bright,
Making morning crazy, quite a sight!

With each segment, jokes unfold,
Golden treasures for the bold.
Tossing peels like confetti rain,
Citrus fun, we’ll entertain!

So munch and crunch, don’t let them sit,
In the mist, we love to commit.
Juicy giggles, don’t you see?
Mandarins always set us free!

The Bright Chords of Citrus

A zesty tune in every slice,
Citrus sun, oh how nice!
Oranges sing, lemons play,
Lemons and laughter start the day.

A grapefruit winks with juicy glee,
Sipping juice, it’s plain to see.
Citrus laughter fills the air,
Every sip, a citrus affair.

In this orchards' musical spree,
Grapes roll by, trying to be.
But the citrus steals the show,
Bright chords shimmer, watch them glow!

So raise your glass and give a cheer,
For citrus joy, let’s all revere.
Squeeze your lemons, shake the jar,
Join the concert, be a star!

Sunlit Citrus Joy

Sunlit citrus makes us grin,
Bright flavors twirl, let’s begin!
Lemons, limes in a playful dance,
Juicy tricks, oh what a chance!

Tangerines laugh, roll around,
In this sunlight, fun is found.
Sour magic, sweet delight,
Citrus capers take flight!

With each sip, a silly cheer,
Ode to drinks that draw us near.
Strawberries jealous, green with rage,
Citrus steals the lively stage!

So raise your glass to sunny days,
Citrus joy in funky ways.
In this garden, smiles abound,
Citrus laughter knows no bound!

Sunshine in Juices

Lemon drops and orange peels,
They dance around in tangy reels,
A splash of zest, a twisty grin,
We sip the sun, let the fun begin!

Limes backflip, grapefruits spin,
In this wild fruit carnival, we all win,
Sucking straws like giddy kids,
With fruity giggles, our joy finally bids!

Pineapple prances, mango sings,
In this bright world where laughter springs,
A citrus chorus, sweet and spry,
We sip and sway, and oh my, oh my!

So let's raise a glass to the zestful cheer,
In this juicy kingdom, we hold so dear,
Where humor drips from every squeeze,
Join the fun, let's giggle with ease!

Chords of Citrus Bliss

Fruits play notes, a juicy band,
Oranges strumming, lemons stand,
Twist and twirl in sunny tunes,
Dancing wildly 'neath the moons!

Lemonades and limey licks,
Singing songs with quirky tricks,
In this symphony of sweet delight,
Citrusy giggles fill the night!

A tangerine’s tone, a grapefruit's beat,
Jiving happily, what a treat!
Chords of joy in every sip,
Join the fruit parade, let’s take a trip!

So let’s toast to flavors that make us grin,
With every drop, let the fun begin,
In this citrus concert, come take a seat,
Where laughter and juice blend oh so sweet!

Citrus Ballad of the Breeze

A breeze of zest, so fresh and bright,
Citrus whispers, oh what a sight!
Lemon trees sway, full of grace,
While oranges giggle, cheeks aglow with mace!

Grapefruits grumble, and squishy lime,
They dream of fun, one slice at a time,
In this ballad filled with glee,
Nature's laughter flows free as can be!

Riding the winds, with citrus flair,
Clouds of fruit scatter everywhere,
We chase the zest, a merry chase,
With juice all over, smiles on every face!

Bubbles in the breeze, oh what a show,
Sipping sunshine, let the rhythm flow,
Join the melody, it’s a citrus fest,
In this whirlwind of fruit, we are truly blessed!

The Dance of Citrus Slices

Sliced fruits twirling, oh what delight,
Lemon pirouettes, dancing in light,
Orange slices prance, with zestful kicks,
Grooving to laughter, with fruity tricks!

Pineapples strut in golden flair,
While grapefruits boogie without a care,
Juicy ballet in a fruity hall,
A slip and a slide, oh, we might fall!

Tangerines cartwheel, a citrus spree,
Bouncing and giggling, wild and free,
Spinning in circles, they spin out of sight,
Dancing with shadows in the moonlight!

So let’s join the dance in this juicy fest,
Where fruits take the lead and we laugh the best,
With citrus slices, life’s pure chance,
Let’s twirl, swirl and do the fruit dance!

Slices of Harmony

Lemons dance in fray, so bright,
Oranges roll with all their might.
Limes in tuxedos, strut with flair,
Citrus chaos fills the air.

Grapefruits giggle, oh what a sight,
Pineapples join in, just for a bite.
Juicy jests fly, zestfully bold,
In this fruit fest, laughter unfolds.

Where pomelos prance, and tangelos twirl,
Every slice spins, every peel curls.
Citrus symphony, sweet and absurd,
In this fruity world, let's spread the word!

Squeeze the day, let the flavors dance,
With zesty humor, take a chance.
Citrus slices, bright and funny,
In every laugh, there's joy, like honey.

Sunkissed Citrus Melodies

Lemon-lovers meet at dawn,
With orange hats and faces drawn.
We're a band of fruit, can't you see?
Playing tunes of zest and glee.

Tangerines roll, singing soft,
While lime's got jokes that lift us aloft.
Grapefruit joins with a tart little ditty,
Together we make the day more witty.

A choir of citrus, bright and round,
Jokes fly high, laughter unbound.
Peels in the air, what a delightful show,
As we zippity-zap to and fro!

Under the sun, our laughter grows,
In this infectious joy, let the sweetness flow.
Sunkissed shenanigans come out to play,
Let's wring out the fun, day after day.

Citrus Tapestry

A tapestry woven with colors bright,
Citrus threads dancing in pure delight.
Lemons laugh, oranges cheer,
In this blend, we shed our fear.

Tales of tang and juicy fray,
Pineapples chuckle, leading the way.
Every fruit a story, woven tight,
In our zesty fabric, we take flight.

Peeling layers, a burst of laughter,
Citrus antics, we won't know the after!
With every twist, spritz, and toss,
We're a fruity workforce, never at a loss.

In this citrus collage, fun reigns supreme,
Each slice a note, each bite a dream.
Tapestry of joy, so colorful and bright,
In our fruity realm, we dance through the night.

Flavors of Fellowship

Gather round, my fruity friends,
We're here for fun, not just amends.
A citrus crew, carving their way,
With laughter as sweet as a summer's day.

Lemon lollipops, oh what a treat,
Orange jokes that can't be beat.
Limes squeeze in with their witty glares,
While silly grapefruits jostle in pairs.

Sharing flavors, a colorful spree,
Tasting joy, oh can't you see?
In every bite, a chuckle awaits,
Fellowship blooms, and laughter creates.

So slice up the fun, let's make a toast,
To fruity friendships we love the most.
In this zestful gathering, spirits arise,
With flavors of laughter, we reach for the skies.

Whirling Zest

Lemons in hats dance a jig,
Oranges in socks, oh so big!
Limes crack jokes with a twisty grin,
Mangoes laugh, let the fun begin.

Juicy tales in zesty sound,
Citrus critters all around.
A grapefruit slips, falls on a peel,
Chortles echo, that's the deal!

Tangerines sing, they're quite a sight,
Their citrus chorus gives pure delight.
Squeezing joy from every fruit,
Giggles rise in this fruity pursuit.

With every splash of tangy zest,
These fruity friends, they're at their best!
In this world of colors bright,
Lemon-laughter brings delight.

Citrus Chords Beneath the Sky

Under a sun so bright and bold,
Limes play tunes that never get old.
With every note, a peel takes flight,
Citrus music fills the night.

Pineapples strum with their leafy hand,
Grapefruits join, forming a band.
Twangy pings from oranges burst,
Laughter ripples, quenches our thirst.

Lemons roll with each jazzy beat,
In this fiesta, there’s no defeat.
Dance away with zestful cheer,
Citrus chords fill the atmosphere!

Squeeze those lemons, let’s take a turn,
Twisting rhymes make our hearts yearn.
Under the stars, they play all night,
Citrus chords, oh what a sight!

Radiant Zest

In a garden of fruits where silliness grows,
Citrus critters wear bright clothes.
Sunshine smiles with sparkly rays,
The fruits break into hilarious plays.

Oranges bounce, like rubber balls,
While lemons giggle, causing downfalls.
Lemonade rivers, sweet and refreshing,
Citrus laughter is so contagious and pressing.

With every squeeze, a chuckle is shared,
The zesty fun shows how much we cared.
Radiant moments we hold so dear,
Fruity joy brings everyone near.

So raise a glass, let's toast to the zest,
With every sip, we feel so blessed.
In this fruity fiesta, we all invest,
Life's a laugh when you're truly zest!

Citrus Vibes

Citrus vibes afloat in the air,
Juggling fruits without a care.
Flying lemons, oranges in flight,
Bouncing limes through day and night.

Dance like a peel that's slipped and spun,
Fruity pranks, oh what fun!
Giggling nectarines join the play,
Creating mischief throughout the day.

Limes drop jokes, they're quite the jest,
Grapefruits roll; they're the best dressed.
Tom-foolery flies with every laugh,
Zentrum zest ignites every path.

So under bright skies, let's all embrace,
The citrus chaos in every space.
Vibrant tales of laughter ignite,
With zesty spirits, we take flight!

Zestful Echoes

Lemon drops fall from the skies,
Orange giggles chase butterfly flies.
A lime’s twist in the jingle too,
Makes everyone dance in the dew.

Grapefruit jokes on citrus trees,
Sourness tickles with a tease.
Tangerines laugh, ‘What’s your name?’
In this zesty, fruity game!

Pineapples wearing socks so bright,
Dancing in the moon's soft light.
Mangoes sway with carefree cheer,
While fruit flies drift in the atmosphere.

Juice boxes sing a silly tune,
Bouncing like a cartoon raccoon.
When fruits combine, oh what a sight,
A merry party through the night!

Melodies of Tangy Sunsets

Sunset spoons in the orange sky,
Lemons leap as they pass by.
Juicy notes on a breezy breeze,
Make the neighbors say, "Oh please!"

Citrus chords on a ukulele,
Dancing ants in their own ballet.
Slice of pie, with an orange twist,
A fruit fiasco you can't resist!

The grapefruit's hat gets blown away,
Spinning circles in the fray.
Lime wedges play the tambourine,
What a sight, it's quite the scene!

As the sun dips, the fruits unite,
Playing pranks in the fading light.
Banana peel slippery delight,
Laughter echoes into the night!

Citrus Serenade

A chorus of peels in the summer air,
Lemons and limes without a care.
Chasing giggles and silly dreams,
In this orchard, nothing's as it seems.

Clementines rolling in a race,
Tangerines grinning, what a face!
Grapes swing from the leafy vines,
Making friends with fruity pines.

Juicy tales from the orange clan,
Bounce around like a playful plan.
Kiwis break into a song,
All together, where we belong.

The berries blurt out goofy puns,
As the kids play hopscotch and runs.
With every peel, the laughter grows,
In this serenade, joy just flows!

Whispers in the Orchard

Soft whispers between the trees,
A playful breeze brings fruity tease.
Peachy secrets shushed in delight,
Waiting for the stars to ignite.

The late-night crew of lemon sprites,
Tickling leaves in the moonlit nights.
Citrus jokes, each cheeky laugh,
Bring bright smiles with every quaff.

Navel oranges plan their schemes,
Twisting tales that burst like dreams.
Mandalay fruit tells ghostly tales,
In the shadows, laughter prevails.

As morning breaks, the sun will shine,
Citrus giggles in every line.
With joyful peels and fruity cheer,
The orchard laughs, “We’ll see you here!”

Notes from the Lemon Grove

In the grove, a lemon danced,
Wobbling, prancing without a chance.
"Hey there, lime! Let’s start a band,"
Together, they made quite a stand.

With zest they played on citrus drums,
All the fruits joined with happy hums.
Grapefruits rolled in, what a sight!
Making music late into the night.

Oranges swung in with a twirl,
Juggling juice as they gave a whirl.
Each note was sweet, each laugh was loud,
In their fruity home, they were proud.

A lemon solo made them cheer,
“Let’s squeeze the day!” they shouted near.
The grove became a stage so bright,
A fruity show, pure delight!

Juicy Silhouettes

In the twilight, silhouettes play,
Fruits in the shadows making sway.
A lemon swoops, a lime spins free,
Dancing shadows, a fruity spree.

Bananas slip in, doing the twist,
While oranges juggle, they can’t be missed.
They slide and glide, bright under the moon,
With fruity laughter, they all croon.

“Who knew the night could be so slick?”
Pineapples laugh, they’ve got the trick.
Each fruit together, a sweet charade,
In the night’s glow, their antics displayed.

Juicy friendships blooming with glee,
In silhouette dances, wild and free.
Under the stars, they make a scene,
A comical, fruity, vibrant dream!

Sunshine in Every Peel

Peeling back layers, a funny sight,
Each fruit's giggles, pure delight.
Peels on the ground, they slip and slide,
With slippery laughter, they can't hide.

Lemons roll and giggle with glee,
"Catch me if you can, come see!"
Tangerines tumble, all in a pile,
Joking and laughing, gone in a while.

With sunny smiles, they make the best,
Dancing around like they're on a quest.
Each little blunder brings more cheer,
In this circus of fruits, they revere.

With every peel, there's joy to add,
"Life's too short, just be glad!"
Under the sun, they'll spin and wheel,
In their silly game, there's joy to feel!

A Melodic Harvest

Harvest time in the orchard bright,
Lemonade breezes, such a delight.
With every pluck, a giggle escapes,
As fruits create their playful shapes.

“Pick me first!” cries a cheeky pear,
“Or I’ll roll away without a care!”
Grapes all chuckle, “We’ll come along,
Let’s make a song as we pick and throng!”

Baskets overflow with juicy cheer,
Each fruit grinning, nothing to fear.
With fun and laughter, the harvest grows,
All around, each fruit bestows.

A fruity jig beneath the sun,
With every harvest, they just have fun.
In this melodic, juicy parade,
Laughter lingers, memories made!

Tangy Harmonies

A lemon and a lime did dance,
In a zesty, fruity trance.
They twirled on a citrus stage,
Jiving with a fruity rage.

Orange joined the crazy fun,
Squeezed the juice, then quickly spun.
Grapefruit winked, said, "Here I am!"
"Pop a twist, and shout, oh sham!"

The crowd of fruits began to sing,
A chorus fit for a king.
Pineapple chimed, all bright and bold,
While bananas danced, so uncontrolled.

In this fruity jamboree,
They laughed and rolled in harmony.
A citrus band of sheer delight,
Playing tunes into the night.

The Scent of Sunshine

A zippy zest fills the air,
As fruits unite in sweet affair.
Lemons chuckle, oranges grin,
As the sunbeams dance within.

The grapefruit's jokes are quite absurd,
Every punchline leaves them stirred.
Mandarins giggle in delight,
Their laughter echoes, pure and bright.

Key limes toss a witty line,
Twirling 'round like they're divine.
Plump little berries cheer them on,
In this perfumed citrus lawn.

The scent of sunshine sticks around,
While fruity melodies abound.
Every slice, a funny cheer,
What a time to be right here!

Citrus Serenade at Dusk

As the sun begins to snuggle,
Citrus fruits delight and chuckle.
Underneath a tangerine sky,
They hum their song, oh my, oh my!

Lemons twirl on a stage of grass,
Kumquats giggle as they pass.
“Let’s dance till the stars appear,”
Squeezed out laughter fills the sphere.

A riff of orange floats the breeze,
While grapefruits tease and aim to please.
Sips of juice spill on nearby ground,
As titters of joy swirl all around.

With twilight cloaked in citrus dreams,
They banter, giggle, and plot schemes.
Under dusk, their laughter sways,
In this zesty, blushing haze.

Lemon Lullabies

Under the moon's bright beam,
The lemons weave a funny dream.
With giggles soft and sweet,
They hum a tune with silly beats.

“Close your eyes, don’t you fret,
Our lullabies aren’t done yet!”
Little citrus, snug and tight,
Bursting forth with pure delight.

Grapefruits snore with all their might,
While tangerines twinkle bright.
A tangy breeze flows in the night,
Lulling fruits till morning light.

So, let the moonlight shine above,
On fruity dreams wrapped in love.
With every laugh and every sigh,
Dancing under the starry sky.

Citrus Poetry of the Sun

Lemons dance in skirts so bright,
Oranges giggle, quite a sight.
With zesty pranks, they roll and play,
Making juice in a splishy-splashy way.

Limes wear hats made of fine zest,
Grapefruits sing, they're simply the best.
In the sun, they sway and bop,
A fruity party that won't stop!

Tangerines roll down the hill,
Squeezing laughter, what a thrill!
With each burst, they crack a joke,
In this orchard, fun's no hoax.

Citrus friends on a merry spree,
Spraying smiles, bursting glee.
With every sip, a sweet surprise,
Their joyful antics never die.

Melodies of Orchard Shadows

In the grove where shadows play,
Lemons strum on a sunny tray.
Grapefruits tickle with their peels,
Creating tunes no one conceals.

Oranges hop on twiggy strings,
Filling air with jolly sings.
Limes join in with a zesty beat,
Dancing fruit is quite the treat!

With every pluck, a giggle springs,
Mandarins share their juicy flings.
Mellow tunes, oh what a sound,
In this orchard, joy is found.

Comical shadows, fruits all sway,
As music molds the sunny day.
With every note, the laughter swells,
An orchard dance, where humor dwells.

Tangy Tales

Once a lemon with a grin,
Told a tale that made us spin.
With each twist, it burst with charm,
An orange winked, 'Oh, what a harm!'

Limes gathered 'round for fun and flair,
Snickering at the juicy scare.
Mandarins swung on branches high,
Sharing secrets to the sky.

Grapefruits fumbled in a joke,
Spitting pulp with every poke.
In this fruity, funny plight,
Each story mixed, a wild delight.

So gather round, let laughter weave,
In tangy tales, you won’t believe.
A slice of humor, fresh and sweet,
In the orchard, life’s a treat.

Citrus Glow

In twilight's shine, the oranges gleam,
With zestful laughter, they dream a dream.
Lemon lights flicker, a funny show,
Under the moon, they dance and glow.

Grapefruits giggle, oh so bright,
Playing hide-and-seek in the night.
With every peel, they shed a grin,
Whispering jokes on the gentle wind.

Limes hop along, bright as the moon,
Fruity tunes make the orchard swoon.
With piquant puns and funny schemes,
They fill the night with zesty dreams.

Citrus glow, a laughter spree,
Where all the fruits are wild and free.
With each flash, they share their cheer,
A glowing night, let's all come near!

www.ingramcontent.com/pod-product-compliance
Lightning Source LLC
Chambersburg PA
CBHW051734290426
43661CB00123B/291
* 9 7 8 1 8 0 5 8 6 4 1 3 4 *